Lots of dots

Nat's top has red dots.

Meg's bag has a big dot.

A big bug has ten dots.

Dan has dots on his bun.

Sam hops on the dots.

Tim has no dots but...

his pup has lots of dots.

Lots of dots   **Level 2, Set 2: Story 16**

Before reading

Say the sounds: g o b h e r f u l

Practise blending the sounds: lots dots Nat's top red Meg's bag dot ten bug Dan bun Sam hops Tim pup

High-frequency words: a big on but   **Tricky words:** of has his the no
Vocabulary check: bun – a small cake

Story discussion: What kind of creature is in the cover picture? Can you think of anything else that has dots?

Teaching points: Check that children can say the phonemes /g/ /o/ /b/ /h/ /e/ /r/ /u/ /l/, and that they can identify the grapheme that goes with each phoneme.
Check that children can sum up what the book is about, and identify what the different things in the story have in common.
Check that children can identify and read the tricky words: of, has, his, the, no.

After reading

Comprehension:
- What colour is Meg's big dot?
- Who has dots on their top?
- Who does the dog belong to?
- Can you think of anything else that has dots that isn't in the book?

Fluency: Speed-read the words again from the inside front cover.